Spot the Differences

Picture Puzzles for Kids

BOOK 2

PHOTO ALTERATIONS BY
SARA JACKSON

DOVER PUBLICATIONS, INC.
MiNeoLa, New York

Bibliographical Note

Spot the Differences Picture Puzzles for Kids 2 is a new work, first published
by Dover Publications, Inc., in 2017.

International Standard Book Number

ISBN-13: 978-0-486-78249-2
ISBN-10: 0-486-78249-2

Manufactured in the United States by LSC Communications
78249202
www.doverpublications.com

Inside this book you'll find twenty-five spot-the-differences challenges. Each puzzle contains two brightly colored photographs—the page on the left contains the original picture, while the page on the right adds 10–15 changes for you to find. Try your best to complete each puzzle on your own—check boxes are provided to help you track your progress—but if you get stuck, just turn to the Answers section, which begins on page 54.

Lemonade
50$

Keep Score: 12 Changes ☐ ☐ ☐ ☐ ☐ ☐ ☐ ☐ ☐ ☐ ☐ ☐ ㉕

Pages 4 - 5

1. Eyeglasses added
2. Spoon changed
3. Buckle removed from strap
4. Sunflower design added
5. Drink color changed
6. Lemon added
7. Cents sign changed
8. Tear in tablecloth added
9. Wood piece added
10. Foot and sandal removed
11. Mouse added

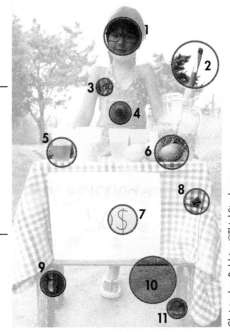

Christopher Robbins ©ThinkStock.com

Pages 6 - 7

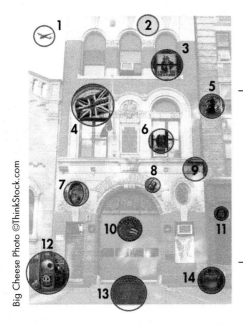

Big Cheese Photo ©ThinkStock.com

1. Airplane added
2. Gargoyle removed
3. Poster added
4. American flag changed
5. Hole in wall added
6. Sculpture added
7. Fish in window added
8. 55 changed to 35
9. Outside light removed
10. Eagle decal added
11. Words added
12. Trash can changed
13. Hopscotch game added
14. Barrel added

Pages 8 - 9

1. Party hat changed
2. Blue shirt changed
3. Cupcake removed
4. Musical note added
5. Couch leg removed
6. Party treats changed
7. Large 5 candle added
8. Pizza added
9. Cupcake added
10. Pink balloon changed
11. Chair leg removed

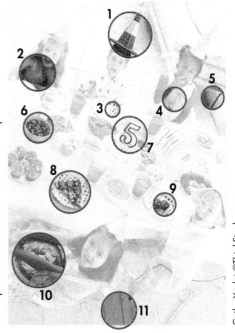

Cathy Yeulet ©ThinkStock.com

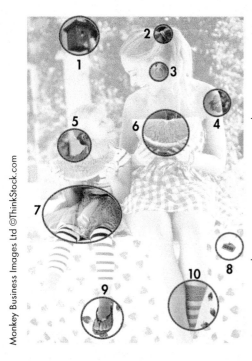

Pages 10 - 11

1. Birdhouse added
2. Black hair band changed
3. Earring added
4. Tattoo added
5. Ponytail removed
6. Watermelon slice changed
7. Pink tutu changed
8. Strawberry changed
9. Sandal added
10. Sock added

Monkey Business Images Ltd ©ThinkStock.com

Pages 12 - 13

1. Moon added
2. Red color changed
3. Bolt removed
4. Girl's leg removed
5. Emoji design added
6. Pants color changed
7. Sunglasses added
8. Rung removed
9. Yellow T connector removed
10. Base of jungle gym changed
11. Shadow changed

katkov ©ThinkStock.com

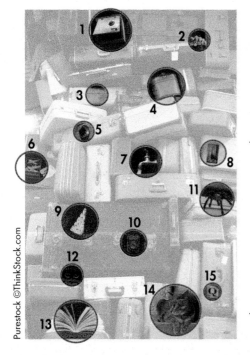

Pages 14 - 15

1. Safe added
2. Hand added
3. Handle removed
4. Suitcase color changed
5. Handle changed
6. Airplane decal added
7. Faucet added
8. Venezia decal added
9. Decal changed
10. Suitcase lock added
11. Tarantula added
12. Cat's eyes added
13. Book added
14. Cat added
15. M decal changed to Q

Purestock ©ThinkStock.com

Pages 16 - 17

1. Picture in frame changed
2. Air conditioner added
3. Face changed
4. Television picture added
5. Shirt color changed
6. Cat added
7. Dog's ear removed
8. Dog's nose changed
9. Y-shaped Lego® removed
10. Legos® added
11. Black fur added
12. Design on carpet removed

Big Cheese Photo ©ThinkStock.com

Pages 18 - 19

1. Bricks removed
2. Face on pumpkin removed
3. Eye patch added
4. Light removed
5. Girl's hand removed
6. Eye black removed
7. Number changed
8. Pumpkin smile changed
9. Dress color changed
10. Pumpkin changed
11. Brick color changed
12. Candy added

Comstock Images ©ThinkStock.com

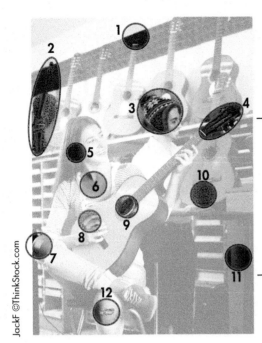

Pages 20-21

1. Guitar head removed
2. Guitar changed
3. Hat added
4. Guitar head color changed
5. Girl's ear covered
6. Necklace removed
7. Bandage added
8. Finger added
9. Doughnut added
10. Design added
11. Outlet added
12. Rip in jeans added

JackF ©ThinkStock.com

Pages 22-23

1. Line added
2. Staircase added
3. Color changed
4. Milk splash added to top of blue vase
5. Photo changed
6. Blue jar changed
7. Design added
8. Necklace added
9. Clock changed
10. Design on teapot removed
11. Toy added
12. Rotary phone changed
13. Block removed

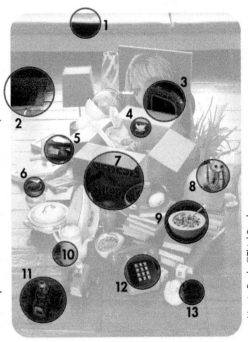

Martin Poole ©ThinkStock.com

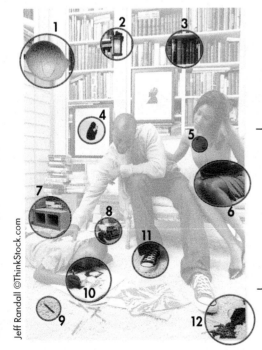

Pages 24-25

1. Lamp changed
2. Light added
3. Bookcase divider removed
4. Picture changed
5. Piece of necklace removed
6. Dress color changed
7. Toy blocks changed
8. Toy truck added
9. Red pencil added
10. Drawing changed
11. Sneaker color changed
12. Wine spill added

Jeff Randall ©ThinkStock.com

Pages 26 - 27

1. Arm added
2. Microphone changed
3. Photo removed
4. Autograph removed
5. Sunglasses added
6. Photo changed
7. Pillow color changed
8. Knee-high sock changed
9. Alarm clock added
10. Dress strap removed
11. Design added

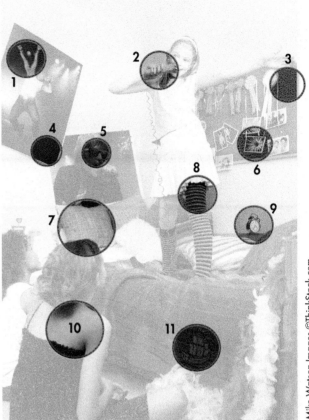

Mike Watson Images ©ThinkStock.com

Pages 28 - 29

1. Clock added
2. Red nose removed
3. Noisemaker changed
4. Man's ear changed
5. Cake changed
6. Tie changed
7. Belt changed
8. Pen added
9. Party hat changed
10. Empty cup filled
11. Pencil removed
12. Message added
13. Plate color changed

Purestock ©ThinkStock.com

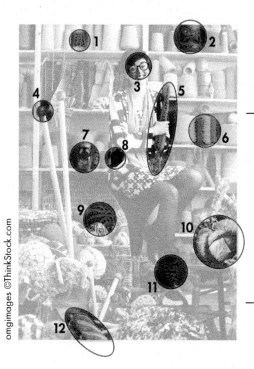

omgimages ©ThinkStock.com

Pages 30 - 31

1. Yarn changed
2. Face added to yarn
3. Eyeglasses added
4. Knob changed
5. Giant knitting needles changed
6. Yarn color changed
7. Jar of change added
8. White square removed from dress
9. White ball of yarn changed
10. Brown ball of yarn changed
11. Shoelace color changed
12. Yarn changed

Pages 32 - 33

1. Stripes changed
2. Balloon hat color changed
3. Letter O changed to E
4. Drawing of can changed
5. Clown's hair color changed
6. Sunglasses changed
7. Bowtie added
8. Necklace removed
9. Cotton candy changed
10. Baseball glove added
11. Trim on dress removed
12. Sewer cover added

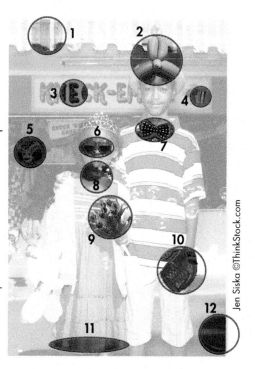

Jen Siska ©ThinkStock.com

Creatas Images ©ThinkStock.com

Pages 34 - 35

1. Treehouse added
2. Sideburn added
3. Butterfly added
4. Hamburger added
5. Design removed
6. Pigeon added
7. Eyeglasses added
8. Earring added
9. Hot dog removed
10. Gray stripe removed
11. Salt shaker added
12. Ear of corn changed

Pages 36-37

1. Large lollipop changed
2. Small piñata added
3. Cork lid changed
4. Label added
5. Red lid changed
6. Smiley face added
7. Lollipop changed
8. Gumball color changed
9. Red candy changed
10. Purple jelly bean removed
11. Striped candy added

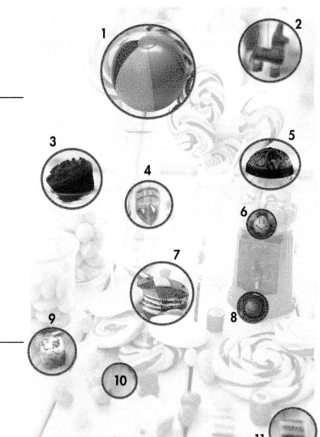

picalotta ©ThinkStock.com

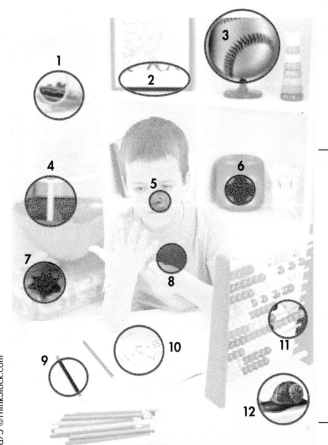

Pages 38-39

1. Hot dog added
2. Green grass removed from picture
3. Globe changed
4. Yellow piece removed
5. Nose earring added
6. Center dot removed
7. Red bow added
8. Thumb removed
9. Pencil removed
10. Addition problem added
11. Yellow beads added
12. Snail added

ilona75 ©ThinkStock.com

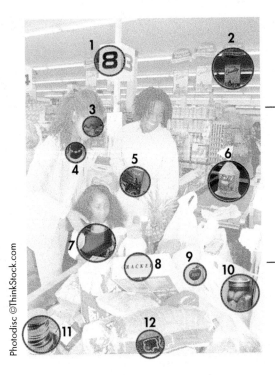

Photodisc ©ThinkStock.com

Pages 40 - 41

1. Number 3 changed to 8
2. Store sign added
3. Eyeglasses added
4. Necklace added
5. Package changed
6. Bag of ice added
7. Dress color changed
8. The word CRACKERS added
9. Juice label added
10. Jar of pickles added
11. Jar of pickles changed
12. Logo added

Pages 42 - 43

1. Telephone added
2. Earmuffs added
3. Ear covered with hair
4. Arm bracelet added
5. Dog design added
6. Cookie removed
7. Tip of icing bag changed
8. Cookie changed
9. Red licorice laces changed
10. Heart design changed
11. Red buttons removed
12. Glittery ball color changed
13. Signature added
14. Cookie piece removed

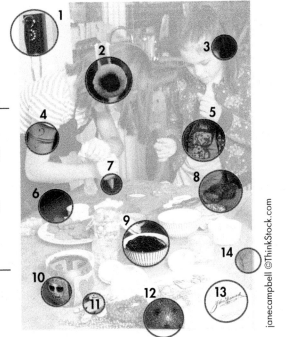

janecampbell ©ThinkStock.com

LeeTorrens ©ThinkStock.com

Pages 44 - 45

1. Teapot reversed
2. Star added
3. Vintage soccer ball changed
4. Letter G changed to R
5. Coffee mug added
6. Toy bus color changed
7. Blue stripe removed
8. The word BUTTER removed
9. Silver bell added
10. The word CLUB added
11. Design changed
12. Hamburger added

Pages 46 - 47

1. Chalkboard diagram changed
2. Letter C changed to D
3. Hair band color changed
4. Book cover color changed
5. Number 9 added
6. Silver eyepiece changed
7. Continent added to globe
8. Beads color changed
9. Finger added
10. False teeth added
11. Toy alligator added
12. Orange marker removed

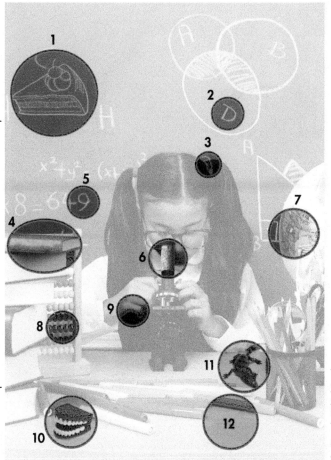

idealistock ©ThinkStock.com

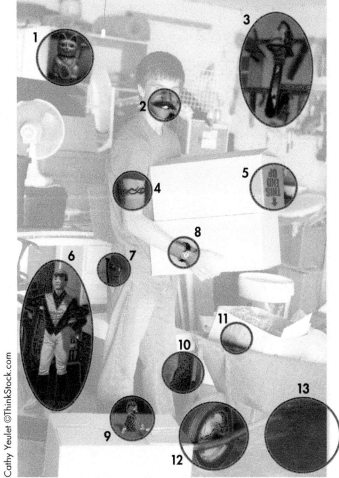

Cathy Yeulet ©ThinkStock.com

Pages 48 - 49

1. Cat statue added
2. Mustache added
3. Chainsaw added
4. Tattoo added
5. Writing on box added
6. Lawn jockey added
7. Wallet added
8. Watch added
9. Puppet added
10. Handle removed
11. Cut-out handle removed
12. Wheel color changed
13. Wheelbarrow stand removed

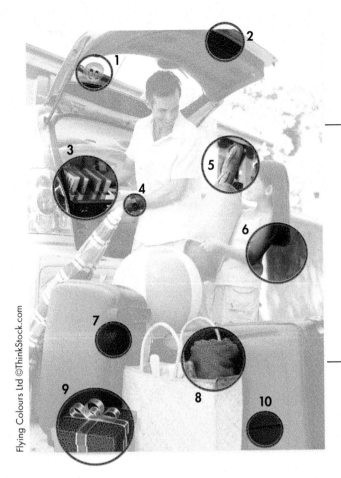

Pages 50 - 51

1. Smiley face decal added
2. Trunk latch removed
3. Duffel bag changed
4. Watch added
5. Beach towel changed
6. Girl's hair changed
7. Luggage stand added
8. Towel color changed
9. Wrapped gift added
10. Luggage zipper added

Flying Colours Ltd ©ThinkStock.com

Pages 52 - 53

1. Pillow design removed
2. Stuffed panda bear changed
3. Watch added
4. Hat on bedpost changed
5. Jewelry case removed
6. Hole added
7. Miniature doors added
8. Jar of cream changed
9. Clothing color changed
10. Sock removed
11. MP3 player changed
12. Polka dot removed
13. Contents of pouch changed

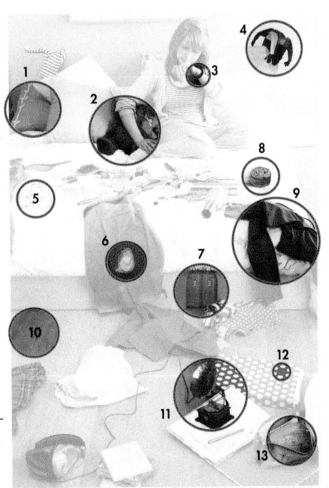

Monkey Business Images ©ThinkStock.com